DIVORCE WITHOUT COURT:

A More Peaceful Solution

© 2021 Vacca Family Law Group

Divorce Without Court: A More Peaceful Solution

All rights reserved. No part of this publication may be reproduced, distributed, or transmitted in any form or by any means, including photocopying, recording, or other electronic or mechanical methods, without the prior written permission of the publisher, except in the case of brief quotations embodied in critical reviews and certain other noncommercial uses permitted by copyright law. For permission requests, contact: info@vaccalaw.com

Published by Vacca Family Law Group
60 E. 42nd Street, Suite 764
New York, NY 10165
www.vaccalaw.com

No portion of this book may be reproduced in any form without permission from the publisher, except as permitted by U.S. copyright law. For permissions contact: info@vaccalaw.com

Do you assume divorce pits one spouse against the other, resulting in a nasty battle where no one actually wins and children are the collateral damage?

When most people think of divorce, they envision a courtroom slugfest and a process that drags on for years, resulting in serious financial problems, unhappy children, and lifelong resentment towards their spouse.

This is not how your divorce has to be.

Yes, divorce is absolutely a painful, emotional process. Your relationship is ending and you're trying to build a future without your spouse. There's a lot that needs to be decided, but the truth is that you can end your marriage in a way that minimizes conflict, is civilized, and lets you both walk away with a doable plan for the future.

If you want to have a non-adversarial divorce, stay out of court and choose **collaborative divorce** or **divorce mediation** instead. These alternatives help you end your marriage, resolve all of the financial issues before you, determine custody of your children, and allow you and your spouse to move forward in the best possible way – with respect, empathy, and good wishes for each other, without going to war.

CONTENTS

About Andrea	1
Forward	3
Why Is Divorce Seen as Adversarial?	7
What is Divorce Really About?	9
What Are My Options if I Want to Keep My Divorce Out of Court?	11
Divorce Mediation	12
Issues Resolved by Mediation	12
The Basics of Divorce Mediation	12
How Divorce Mediation Works	13
Benefits of Mediation	15
Divorce Mediation Attorneys and Professionals	16
Choosing Divorce Mediation	17
Collaborative Divorce	18
Issues Resolved by Collaborative Divorce	18
The Basics of Collaborative Divorce	18
How Collaborative Divorce Works	19
Collaborative Divorce Attorneys	20
The Collaborative Divorce Team	20
Benefits of Collaborative Divorce	21
Choosing Collaborative Divorce	23
What Are My First Steps to Keep my Divorce Out of Court?	25

About Andrea

Andrea Vacca is a mediator and collaborative lawyer, as well as the founder of Vacca Family Law Group, a firm focusing exclusively on non-adversarial divorce and family law matters.

As a mediator, Andrea helps both her client and their spouse to hear each other, bridge their differences, and arrive at an agreement that works for them. As a collaborative divorce attorney, she strongly advocates for her client without being adversarial or insensitive.

In addition to a B.A. and J.D, Andrea also has a Certificate in Positive Psychology. She uses this revolutionary approach to help her clients navigate their divorces. She fosters a growth mindset, being resilient and encouraging mindfulness.

Andrea is the President of the Board of Directors of the New York Association of Collaborative Professionals. She is also the Associate Director of the National Association of Divorce Professionals as well as a member of many New York professional groups committed to family and divorce mediation.

Andrea regularly lectures, and she writes and blogs on collaborative law, mediation, prenuptial agreements and non-adversarial family law.

After practicing traditional, litigation-focused family law for many years, Andrea knows there is a better, more peaceful way to approach divorce. Her Manhattan firm is committed to helping clients resolve their divorces out of court and feel better prepared to make the decisions they need to move forward, without regret.

Andrea wrote *Divorce Without Court: A More Peaceful Solution* because she wants everyone who is considering divorce to know that it does not have to be a war and that mediation and the collaborative divorce process are much better options.

Andrea is also the author of the chapter on Collaborative Law in the book, *Onward & Upward: A Guide For Getting Through New York Divorce & Family Law Issues.*

She lives in Manhattan with her husband.

Forward

How I Became a Divorce Lawyer
People ask me, "Why did you become a divorce lawyer?" I usually tell people I wanted to work in an area where I could litigate and work with people—as opposed to working with corporations or parcels of land. Family law seemed like a good fit for that. I eventually realized that litigation wasn't the right path for me or my clients. I'm not so much a fighter as I am an advocate. And that's why I left litigation behind and moved to collaborative law and mediation.

That's the short answer.

Drawing On My Parent's Painful Divorce
The long answer is a bit more complicated and has its roots in my childhood. Growing up, it was plain to see that my father and mother had an unhappy marriage. Their pain and sadness were palpable. From the time I was 12 or 13 years old, I regularly asked my mother, "If you're so unhappy, why don't you just get divorced?"

By the time I was a junior in college, they started talking about divorce. I was settling into a semester abroad in Denmark when my mother finally answered my question. Talking to her on the phone in the hallway of my dorm, she blurted out, "I've left your father. I've moved out."

As it turns out, my mother and father had been working with divorce lawyers to come to a settlement agreement. My father was supposed to be the one to move out, but he kept stalling and then refused to follow through. My mother reached a breaking point.

One day while my father was not home, she moved out without telling him. With the help of friends, she packed up her belongings, hired movers, and headed across town to a new home. She broke the news to my 14-year-old brother that afternoon, and had my 20-year-old sister wait for my father when he got home. To put it mildly, this was not a good plan, but my mother was desperate to be separated from my father. This was the only way she thought she could make it happen.

When I heard all of this my heart broke. I thought about my father coming home to an "empty" house. I thought about the frustration, fear, and anxiety that my mother must have felt as she had planned her secretive move. I thought about my brother and sister being put in the middle of the chaos. And there was nothing I could do about any of this as I was in the middle of my once-in-a-lifetime experience in a foreign country for a semester abroad.

Impact of Divorce not Done Well
My parents were eventually able to negotiate an agreement and thankfully kept my siblings and me out of the details of the negotiations. In the end, my mother kept her business. My father kept the family home and rental property.

That seemed fair on paper, but my father told me sometime later that he felt "raped" by my mother. He "agreed" to this division of property but he wasn't happy about it. He had suffered from depression in the past and now it came back with full force.

Over the next year, he basically stopped doing anything. He stopped going to work, he stopped paying the mortgage on both homes, and he eventually filed for bankruptcy. He wasn't alone because my brother was living with him, but even that was a less-than-ideal situation because my parents had let my brother choose who to live with and of course he picked my father, who let him do whatever he wanted. The novelty of that eventually wore off and, within a year, my brother was living with my mother.

Even though my parents came to an agreement out of court, it wasn't done well. Not only did my little brother get bounced around, and not only did my father lose everything he received in the divorce, but my father also did everything he could to avoid looking at my mother for at least 10 years.

At my sister's wedding, he refused to be in photographs with my mother. When that same sister had a child, she would edit my mother out of photos before she would send them to my father. We all knew it was ridiculous for her to enable my father in this way, but even adult children get pulled into the middle of divorce and do what they can to make both parents happy.

A Truce and Time For Healing
During those 10 years, we had all requested of my dad that he rejoin the family at one point or another. I remember saying "Dad, I'm not saying you need to call Mom and be friends, but if there's an event that comes up in the future, I'm requesting that you be a part of our family again."

Two years later, my mother's mother died and my father, without being asked said, "I'm coming." He flew up from

Florida where he was then living, he came to the funeral, he spent time in my grandparents' house after the wake, and he was at the church and cemetery. We had lost my grandmother, but we got my father back. And that was that. For all future major family events, we didn't have to worry about how to deal with parents fighting a cold war.

Unlike my sister who had to coordinate her wedding photos to make sure our parents were separated, when my other sister and I got married, both of my parents walked us down the aisle and we were completely able to feel their mutual love for us rather than their anxiety about having to be so close to the other.

So why did I become a divorce lawyer? If I can help it, I don't want other families to go through what my family went through. It's a waste of time. It hurts. Everyone's in pain. When parents divorce badly, it can last for generations. If they divorce well, that can last for generations too. I want to do whatever I can to help my clients divorce well and for their children to have much different divorce stories than mine.

Why Is Divorce Seen as Adversarial?

The public perception of divorce is that it's complex, crazily expensive, and ultimately emotionally draining. Many people think it's like chemotherapy – it will cure you, but it could almost kill you in the process. It does not have to be that way.

Why does everyone think this, then? A traditional litigated divorce is not a friendly process. One spouse files paperwork with the court asking for a divorce. Those papers are often served on the other spouse in a sneak attack – out of the blue with no warning.

Each person gets a lawyer, and those lawyers start to build their courtroom arguments for why their client should get everything – all the money, all the time with the kids, the home, the retirement accounts, as well as huge amounts of child support and alimony payments. The spouses live in conflict and complete chaos while the attorneys battle it out.

It takes months and months and sometimes years for the case to proceed through the system. Eventually, after many court appearances that take all day and where nothing actually happens, the case goes to trial. Each spouse takes turns saying bad things about each other and tearing each other apart. Each attorney tries to portray the opposite side as evil and cruel.

The judge, who doesn't know either spouse, makes a decision that impacts every aspect of their lives, including how their children will spend time with them and how much money on which they must live. Everyone walks away feeling battered, resentful, angry, and misunderstood.

That's what a traditional, litigated divorce can look like. **You can absolutely avoid this process.** Collaborative divorce and divorce mediation are choices that allow you to end your marriage in a civil and rational way, while actually reducing (not increasing) conflict, all without setting foot in a courtroom or having to plot against your spouse.

What is Divorce Really About?

Divorce is probably one of the most emotional things you'll deal with in your life, but that does not mean it has to be filled with anger. A divorce is a legal end to your marriage, and it resolves all of the financial and parenting issues between you, including:

- How you will share your assets and debts as you move forward, including cash, investments, credit card debt, mortgages, and loans

- What you will do with your marital home, as well as other real property and where you will each live

- How you will divide your household and personal belongings

- Whether one of you will continue to provide financial support for the other spouse after the marriage has ended

- How you will share your retirement assets and plan so you can both retire comfortably in the future

- And if you have children, how you will share time with them and financially support them

When you choose a non-adversarial divorce, you and your spouse work through every single one of these issues in a thoughtful manner and reach conclusions together in a calm and reasonable setting.

Together, you will make each decision and work out the details so that the resulting divorce plan will fit both of your lives and benefit your children. Your divorce does not involve courtroom drama, scheming against each other, or money grabs.

What Are My Options if I Want to Keep My Divorce Out of Court?

If you and your spouse want to maintain control of your divorce, proceed at a pace you set, and make decisions yourselves that work for your family, there are two main options you should consider. Divorce mediation and collaborative divorce both offer civilized pathways to the end of your marriage that completely avoid court and a trial. These processes help you move through each decision with confidence, support, and respect.

Divorce Mediation

Divorce mediation offers a non-adversarial, cooperative way for you and your spouse to end your marriage and create a resolution for all the issues involved in your divorce. Mediation resolves every issue in your divorce through a process that is thoughtful, creative, and solutions-based. Each mediation is unique and focused on the particular needs that you and your spouse have.

Issues Resolved by Mediation

Divorce mediation offers complete solutions for every issue in your divorce, including:

- Parenting plans and schedules, including legal custody determinations for your children
- Valuation of marital assets
- Division of all marital assets and debts
- Establishment of alimony or spousal support, if necessary
- Creation of child support, if needed

The Basics of Divorce Mediation

In divorce mediation, you and your spouse work with a mediator to resolve all the issues in your divorce.

There are three key elements to divorce mediation:

1. You work with a neutral third-party mediator who helps you and your spouse make all of the decisions before you.

2. You and your spouse get advice from individual attorneys who consult with you and provide support as you move through the process, but who typically are not in the mediation sessions with you.

3. You and your spouse agree to approach the process with honesty and integrity, sharing documents and information with each other and your mediator.

How Divorce Mediation Works

Your non-judgmental mediator guides you through the issues you need to resolve, helping you consider all the options and eventually working with you to achieve resolution of every item in your divorce.

You and your spouse are the negotiators in this scenario, and the mediator helps you learn to work together while overcoming emotional and communication challenges to reach an agreement.

The mediator does not make any decisions or judgments during the process, and instead acts as a guide as you and your spouse collaborate to create personal solutions that fit your family.

Mediators are skilled in jump-starting the process, keeping the lines of communication open, offering options you might not see, and demonstrating and teaching understanding. The mediator is there to ensure you both act fairly and to keep you on track throughout the process.

The mediator meets with both of you at regularly scheduled sessions that are designed to be civil and productive. The focus is on creating solutions and finding common ground, not rehashing the past.

Mediation is not therapy, but it can be therapeutic because it allows you to reach through the clouded atmosphere of your marriage to find an outcome you both are comfortable with.

The mediation process takes the place of a litigated divorce. You agree to work together with the mediator to resolve the issues in your divorce, instead of asking a judge to make those decisions for you.

In addition to the mediator, you each work separately with your own attorney who advises you of your rights, the requirements of the law, and opinions about what kinds of outcomes would be fair and reasonable in your situation. This attorney is available as a sounding board and source of advice throughout the process. However, the attorney typically does not attend the mediation sessions.

The mediation sessions place the power squarely in your and your spouse's hands. You are free to consider whatever you need however you need it, and in whatever order you feel comfortable. The mediator ensures you work together in a safe space. Jointly, you create solutions you both see as feasible, resolving every aspect of the divorce yourselves.

The end result of divorce mediation is a signed separation agreement that incorporates all the decisions you and your spouse have made. The terms become incorporated into the divorce decree. A judge who doesn't understand your family will not be making any decisions for you.

Benefits of Mediation

Mediation offers many benefits, including:

- **Creativity and flexibility.** You and your spouse are free to fashion solutions that work for your unique circumstances, instead of cookie-cutter solutions implemented by a court.

- **Privacy.** All of the discussions and the facts considered in mediation are private and not a matter of public record as they are in a divorce proceeding in court.

- **Cooperation.** The mediation process encourages you and your spouse to work together, communicating directly to reach mutually agreeable outcomes.

- **Child-focused process.** Mediation keeps the needs of the children front and center. The process reduces conflict in your family, teaching both of you how to work together to solve problems, which has a positive impact on children. Mediation also allows you, as parents, to model cooperative behavior for your children.

- **Control.** The mediation process gives you control over the schedule, pacing, and direction of the sessions. It also provides complete control of the outcome of your case, instead of having a judge – who does not understand your family – making decisions.

- **Solution-oriented procedures.** Mediation is focused on finding mutually agreeable solutions, not on increasing conflict and negative emotions.

- **Future skills.** Mediation benefits you not just today, but in the future. In particular, if you are parents, you are likely to face situations in the coming years where you will not see entirely eye-to-eye. Mediation teaches you the skills you need to work through those situations in the future and find compromises.

Divorce Mediation Attorneys and Professionals

Attorneys who practice divorce mediation have a background in divorce and family law and have completed specialized mediation training, but they function only as mediators in their mediation cases.

They will not represent either spouse nor will they litigate the divorce. They are not able to provide legal advice to either spouse but can provide legal information, such as discussing what the law requires.

During your mediation, it may be helpful to work with a divorce financial expert as well. These professionals will help gather and distill the financial information, offer explanations and possible plans to help you deal with any complicated financial aspects of your divorce including how to divide all of your assets, determine what amount of spousal and child support is needed, and advise how to deal with any debts.

Choosing Divorce Mediation

The first step in beginning the cooperative process of divorce mediation is to find a mediator with whom you both feel comfortable. Schedule a consultation with a mediator to ask questions about the process and decide whether they are a good fit for you and your spouse.

Andrea Vacca, Esq. and her team at Vacca Family Law Group are skilled divorce mediators with many years of experience. They approach each mediation with a cooperative, forward-focused strategy and have experience in helping couples find common ground and out-of-the-box solutions at a comfortable pace.

Andrea is the President of the New York Association of Collaborative Professionals and the Associate Director of a New York City chapter of the National Association of Divorce Professionals. Call her today at 212-768-1115 or email her at info@vaccalaw.com.

At this point, you may think mediation sounds like a great option, but you may be concerned that you or your spouse will find it difficult to advocate for yourself in the mediation room. If you believe that one of you will need more support when discussing complex legal, emotional, or financial issues, then you should consider the collaborative divorce process.

Collaborative Divorce

Collaborative divorce allows you and your spouse to resolve every single issue in your divorce without going to court, in a civil and calm process with your attorneys by your side during the negotiations.

This solutions-based approach puts the power in your hands and rests responsibility on each of you equally to act with respect and dignity through each step. In a collaborative divorce, you and your spouse, with attorneys next to you, will work through all the decisions that need to be made in a divorce without the conflict of a courtroom.

Issues Resolved by Collaborative Divorce

Collaborative divorce provides complete resolution for all the issues you face in a divorce, including:

- Parenting plans and schedules, including legal custody designations
- Division of all your marital assets and debts
- Valuation of all marital assets
- Determination about spousal support or alimony payments
- Creation of child support, if necessary

The Basics of Collaborative Divorce

In collaborative divorce, both you and your spouse retain attorneys who are collaborative lawyers. There are three key elements to collaborative divorce:

1. You, your spouse, and your attorneys all agree that you are going to handle your divorce through the collaborative process and will not go to court.

2. You and your spouse agree that you will be honest and open with each other and your attorneys and share information and documents related to the marriage and divorce.

3. You will consider solutions that are designed to create the best possible outcomes for you and your children while considering the needs of the entire family.

How Collaborative Divorce Works

You and your spouse each retain separate attorneys who are designated as collaborative divorce attorneys. Your attorneys work with you to gather all the information necessary to understand your assets, debts, financial situation, and parenting life. Your attorney will spend time with you to help you understand your legal rights, choices, and responsibilities throughout the process.

You, your spouse, and both attorneys meet together at scheduled sessions to carefully and thoughtfully work through each issue that needs to be resolved in the divorce. The meetings are structured with agendas so that everyone knows what will be discussed.

The meetings are handled as careful professional negotiations. Minutes (notes) are made of the sessions so there is a clear statement about what everyone agreed to.

You sign a settlement agreement at the end of the process which lays out all the decisions made. This is then submitted to the court, and the terms are incorporated into your divorce decree. All of the decisions are made directly by you and your spouse, not by a judge who is unfamiliar with your family and situation. The terms of the divorce are controlled completely by you and your spouse, and only things you agree on are included in your decree. You both walk away with newfound freedom, financial resolution, a secure relationship with your children, and a plan for the future.

Collaborative Divorce Attorneys

Attorneys who practice collaborative divorce are committed to resolving divorce cases through negotiation. A collaborative attorney works closely with you through the divorce process, meeting with your spouse and their attorney and providing thoughtful and realistic options and suggestions. The attorneys are committed to the collaborative process and will not take your case to court under any circumstances.

Collaborative attorneys have extensive experience practicing family and divorce law, are trained as mediators, and receive ongoing training in collaborative divorce.

The Collaborative Divorce Team

Collaborative divorce provides the flexibility to consider all of the issues involved in your divorce. It also gives you access to a team of professionals who are trained in collaborative divorce and mediation and are able to help you and your spouse with specific issues and concerns.

- **Family specialists** (also known as divorce coaches). Communication difficulties are common in many divorces. A family specialist is a mental health professional who helps you learn to communicate more clearly with your spouse, both during and after the divorce. This is not therapy. Family specialists provide support, empathy, and feedback as you deal with the complex issues in your divorce.

- **Child specialists.** Your child's concerns and perspectives are important components in the divorce process. A child specialist allows your child's voice and opinion to be heard and considered during the collaborative divorce process.

- **Financial specialists.** Because divorce is heavily a financial transaction, it is worthwhile to work with a financial expert who can help you make educated decisions about your finances. These decisions will include how to value and divide assets and liabilities, what amount of child support or spousal support needs to be paid, and how to address tax issues.

Benefits of Collaborative Divorce

Collaborative divorce has many benefits, making it an excellent choice for you and your family:

- **Team approach.** Working with specialized professionals as part of your collaborative team will address the financial, emotional, and legal aspects in concrete ways so none of those issues overly influence decision-making around another.

- **Personalized pacing.** You can move as quickly or as slowly as you and your spouse need, without a court's timetable to worry about.

- **Cooperative nature.** The collaborative divorce process focuses on working with your spouse, with the assistance of your collaborative attorneys, to resolve your issues together.

- **Solutions-based focus.** Collaborative divorce is focused on finding real and detailed solutions that benefit your family, which is quite different from a litigated divorce that can sometimes create as many problems as it resolves.

- **Child-friendly process.** Because you and your spouse are not pitted against each other, the process is less combative and more peaceful for your children.

- **Creative nature.** The process allows you and your spouse to create schedules, plans, finances, and compromises that are unique and crafted to meet your family's needs.

- **Guided assistance.** Collaborative divorce puts you in a room with your spouse, with your collaborative attorney at your side. You have legal advice at all times and also have the security of having someone who is on your team leading you through the entire process.

- **Control.** Instead of a judge, who does not understand your family, making long-reaching decisions for you, you and your spouse work with your lawyers and the other collaborative professionals to create a plan that takes all of your needs into consideration. Additionally, all the discussions and facts involved in your case are private, under your control, and not part of a court record.

- **Future-facing perspective.** Collaborative divorce allows you to create an agreement that will work today, but also far into the future until your children are grown.

Choosing Collaborative Divorce

When you choose collaborative divorce as your non-adversarial divorce process, it puts control of the process in your hands and allows you to move at your pace, resolving each issue individually with care and thought. Your collaborative attorney works for you and with you, negotiating possible solutions and plans with your spouse and their collaborative attorney.

The process is designed to remove or reduce conflict and focus on finding mutually agreeable resolutions. You have legal representation at your side throughout the entire process. The end result is a complete resolution of your divorce, with a plan for you to move forward into the future.

Andrea Vacca, Esq., and the attorneys at Vacca Family Law Group are experienced collaborative divorce attorneys who work as strong advocates for each of their clients. Their approach is reasonable, calming, and proactive. Andrea is the President of the Board of Directors of the New York Association of Collaborative Professionals and Associate Director of a New York City chapter of the National Association of Divorce Professionals. She is also a member of the International Association of Collaborative Professionals.

Her years of experience give her the insight necessary to guide the process, offer thoughtful solutions, and help her clients make the best choices for their individual needs. She's available to help you with your collaborative divorce case today. Call her at 212-768-1115 or email her at info@vaccalaw.com.

What Are My First Steps to Keep my Divorce Out of Court?

If you want to keep your divorce out of court, talk with your spouse about your options. Show them this ebook or our website. Make it clear you don't want to fight and instead want to work with them to end your marriage. Suggest collaborative divorce or divorce mediation as options that will get you both what you want.

If you want more help finding the right way to speak to your spouse about collaborative divorce, this article can help: How to Talk to Your Spouse about Collaborative Divorce

If you hope to keep your divorce out of court, do not file divorce papers yourself or with an attorney. Instead, set up a meeting with a collaborative divorce or divorce mediation attorney who can help you understand the process and offer suggestions for how to get your spouse on board.

Whether you choose collaborative divorce or divorce mediation, a non-adversarial approach to divorce will benefit everyone in your family and help you end your marriage with as little conflict as possible. Avoiding the drama, high emotions, and impersonal nature of the courtroom and handling your divorce privately will set you on a positive path for the future.

What Comes Next?

Once you and your spouse agree to take a non-adversarial approach to your divorce, it would be a good idea for each of you to find an attorney you trust to guide you through the process. Regardless of whether you opt to use divorce mediation or collaborative divorce, assistance from an attorney who is focused on your priorities could ensure that nothing is left to chance so you can emerge satisfied and ready to move forward.

Remember that even if you keep your divorce out of court, you will still set legal terms that carry just as much weight as those created by a judge. Your negotiated agreements will determine critical factors such as how you will divide up your property, how you will deal with retirement and support, and how you will handle issues affecting your children. Working with an attorney experienced in non-adversarial divorce can make sure that you fully consider all issues before reaching a decision.

At Vacca Family Law Group, we are firmly committed to helping couples achieve the benefits of divorce without court. We would be happy to talk to you about how the process might work in your situation. Call us today at 212-768-1115 or email us at info@vaccalaw.com to schedule a consultation.

www.ingramcontent.com/pod-product-compliance
Lightning Source LLC
Chambersburg PA
CBHW070910220526
45466CB00005B/2185